This book belongs to

First published 2011 by Brown Watson
The Old Mill, 76 Fleckney Road,
Kibworth Beauchamp, Leic LE8 0HG

ISBN: 978-0-7097-1919-9

My First

123

Brown Watson

ENGLAND

1

one boy

2

two cockerels

3

three cars

four rabbits

five balls

6

six ice creams

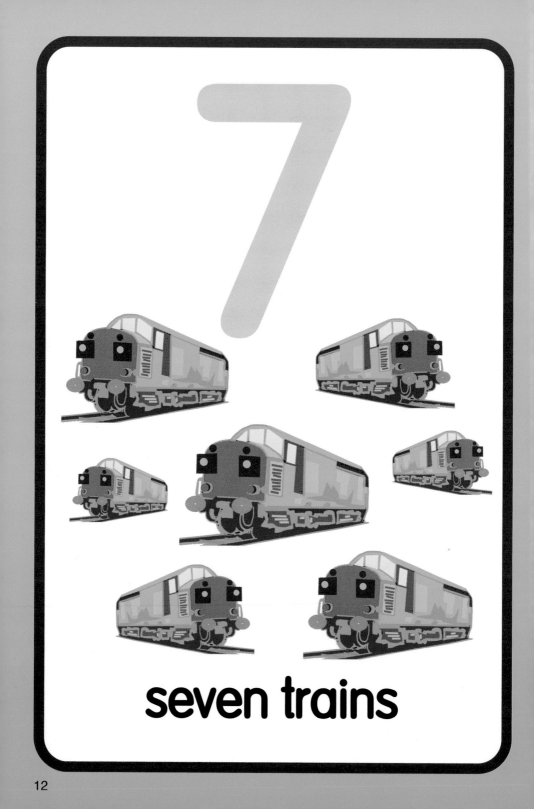

seven trains

8

eight flowers

9

nine babies

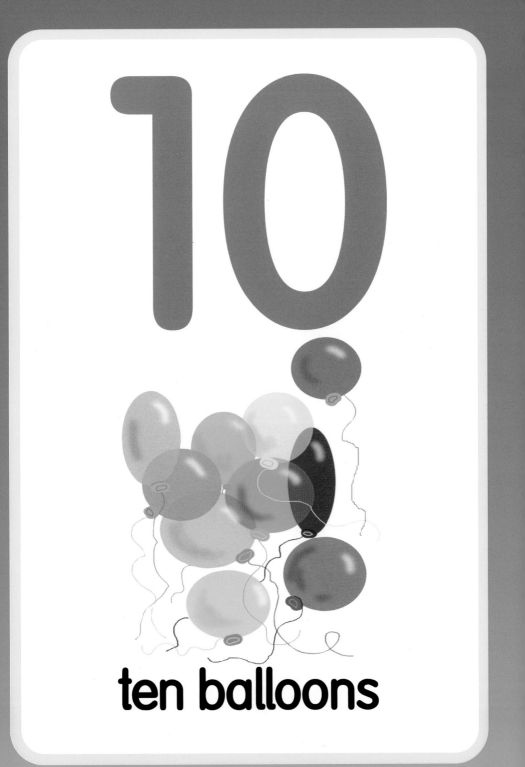

10

ten balloons

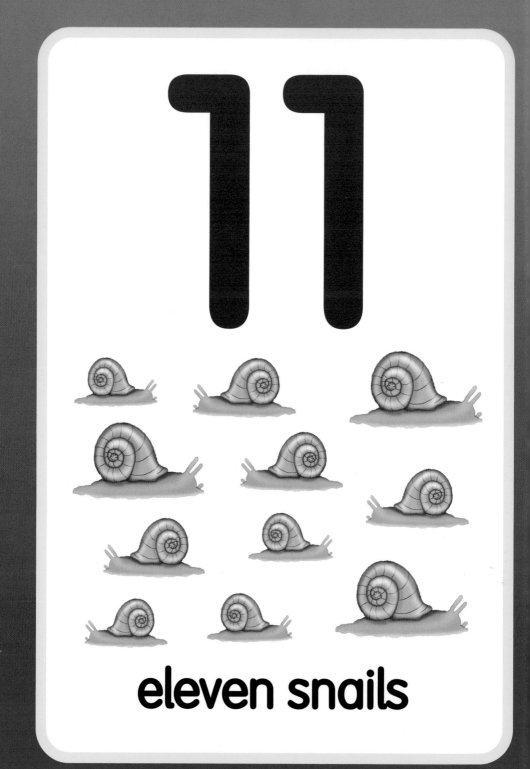

11

eleven snails

twelve stars

thirteen ducks

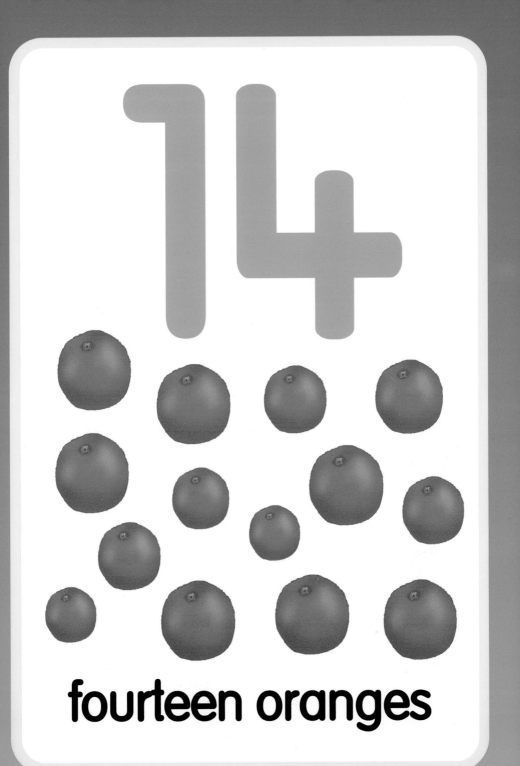

fourteen oranges

15

fifteen kittens

16

sixteen pencils

17

seventeen bees

eighteen shapes

19

nineteen butterflies

20

twenty chicks

1	2	3	4	5
one	two	three	four	five
6	7	8	9	10
six	seven	eight	nine	ten
11	12	13	14	15
eleven	twelve	thirteen	fourteen	fifteen
16	17	18	19	20
sixteen	seventeen	eighteen	nineteen	twenty

How many triangles can you count?
How many squares can you count?

Count the number of circles and stars!

How many pink balloons can you see?